To My GOOD FRI
ENJOY THE
Peter

M000295652

FORD TRANSIT
THE MAKING OF AN ICON

Peter Lee

AMBERLEY

This book is dedicated to Vernon Preston, the true father of the Ford Transit. He started work with Ford in 1942 at the age of seventeen. In 1960 he took control of a project called Redcap, later to be known as the Ford Transit, designing the ground-breaking Uni-body (Uni-body means no chassis). He also came up with the wider front wheelbase to give a better turning circle. Vernon knew his Uni-body innovation would change the industry and this was just the first of a long line of innovations put into place by him and his team on the Redcap project as they overcame the problems during the next five years. He was right; the Transit did change the commercial vehicle market drastically. Vernon was a true gentleman and today, fifty-two years after he started work on the Transit project, there are not many light commercial vehicles of any make on the roads of the world that have not been directly influenced by Vernon's brilliance and his engineering excellence.

Peter George Lee
June 2017

First published 2017

Amberley Publishing
The Hill, Stroud
Gloucestershire, GL5 4EP

www.amberley-books.com

Copyright © Peter Lee, 2017

The right of Peter Lee to be identified as the Author of this work has been asserted in accordance with the Copyrights, Designs and Patents Act 1988.

ISBN 978 1 4456 6782 9 (print)
ISBN 978 1 4456 6783 6 (ebook)

All rights reserved. No part of this book may be reprinted or reproduced or utilised in any form or by any electronic, mechanical or other means, now known or hereafter invented, including photocopying and recording, or in any information storage or retrieval system, without the permission in writing from the Publishers.

British Library Cataloguing in Publication Data.
A catalogue record for this book is available from the British Library.

Origination by Amberley Publishing.
Printed in the UK.

Contents

For me this picture sums up the Transit story in one go. It shows the first month of production at the Langley plant; vans were everywhere as Ford tried to keep up with orders. These are all SVO vehicles in bay 4, police, ambulance and fire along with orders for the armed services. The car park was full up and so was a storage yard 5 miles from the plant. The plant went from one shift to three in a matter of months. All these vans were sent from Southampton and they were queued up there as well.

Introduction

Over the fifty-two years that the Ford Transit van has been on sale, it has pretty much just blended into the general motoring scene; after all, it is just a van-shaped tool to do a job. But when you look into what came before and after this iconic vehicle, it does stand out head and shoulders above the rest as being a revolution in van technology and design in the vehicle engineering industry. It has been the UK's top seller in its class for over fifty-two years and this accolade is also true for parts of Europe and the whole of North America today. A lot of people are under the misapprehension that the story of the Transit started in 1965, give or take a few years, but although it was 1965 when Ford first showed the Transit van to the public, in fact actual planning for the Transit had commenced in 1957. It took three years of highly detailed planning and research to lay the foundations of the Transit, and only then would the project known as the 'V-series', later known as 'Redcap', start. No one knew about the secret eight-year-long project going on in the background before the launch of the Transit, and it all started with a young Ford project planner named Arthur Molyneaux. Arthur was instructed by Henry Ford himself at a meeting in 1957 to carry out the work. Vernon Preston told me, 'It was Arthur's hard work that put myself in such a strong position by letting me know exactly what was needed to be done. Arthur was a genius and his instructions were exact and precise.'

Ford at the time was made up of a group of companies all around the world that was fragmented and losing money. As an example, Ford Germany was testing a new van (Taunus) and Ford UK was also testing a new van (Thames 800E), but project leaders in both countries, just 400 miles apart, did not know that there were two projects underway as very little contact existed between them. Germany designed and built their products and the UK did the same, so there was no reason for dialogue. Henry Ford Junior changed all of this when taking control of Ford World by setting up a competition between both companies. The winner would get the right to build a van for all of Europe, not just part of it. The UK won the right to design the new vehicle – the Ford Transit – and the rest is history, but that was still eight years away. While the project would be completed in secrecy, it would be a joint project by both countries, headed by an American, Ed Baumgartner. In fact, the Transit project was so successful, both financially and from a design point of view, that it led to the formation of Ford Europe in 1967.

It took Arthur until 9 January 1960 (his birthday) before he handed over his planning project ideas to Mr Ford himself at Trafford House (Ford's head office at the time). Arthur showed his wooden buck test platform to the team that would build the van – codenamed the 'V series project', it would later become 'Project Redcap' before being named the Transit just a few weeks before the final test vehicles were put together in May 1965. The engineering team was headed up by Vernon Preston, the chassis and suspension engineer, Dick Morphew, the body designer, and Chris Kope, who was American, but it soon became obvious that Vernon would lead the way with his ground-breaking ideas. The prototype building and testing side of things lasted five years, and it took three months for the pre-production vans to be completed. The team's brilliance at looking at all the old van's design faults and overcoming them was ground-breaking. In fact they were a revolution, in design, engineering and testing techniques; so much so that a lot of their ideas put in place are still incorporated today in commercial vehicle design and testing. The Transit project made Bedford, VW and British Leyland stop their ongoing design projects and refine what they were doing. Arthur told Bedford to purchase three Transits so they could take them apart and see how they worked. From the first month of the Transit being on the market it was the market leader – a position it still holds it today. In September 1965, Ford took £33 million in orders – in today's money that is £600 million worth of sales.

Ford has constantly updated the project during its history. The list of 'firsts' that have been fitted as standard items is quite amazing. From simple things like a side loading door, radio, disk brakes, air conditioning, seat belts, one piece back door, airbags and the first light-van to have seatbelts as standard, through to today's innovations like Bluetooth, lane keeping warning, tyre pressure warning, sat nav, reversing cameras, phone connect capability and central locking. It was the first van to take three euro pallets, and leads the way with crash tests for strength and safety. The list is endless. Over 450 variations exist with the Transit's current models. Door positions, engines, seats, length of chassis, weight and roof heights: these are just some of the factors that make it easy to have a van to fit your requirements. Ford are investing billions worldwide in technology and safety in its best-selling van, making sure the Transit name is top of the list and a name that drivers can trust. That's how you build an icon.

The design and engineer teams from the Redcap program alongside the River Thames on 25 July 1985 celebrating 2 million Transits off the line in Southampton, followed by lunch in the Ford hospitality launch and a river trip. From left to right: Colin Cambell; Colin Clark; Peter Best; Arthur Molyneaux; Fred Ray; Ron Butler; Ed Baumgartner; Vernon Preston; Gerry Clark; Erich Mohr; Stan Gadsden; Phil Ives; Tom Bedwell; Dick Morphew; Brian Eckersley; Non Crook.

The V-Series 1957–1960

Ford Germany were selling the Ford Taunus Transit in very large numbers to companies like Monark. It was a strong van and well built. The body shells were made in a pressing plant a few miles away from the assembly plant and shipped down the river Rhine to be put together. German commercial vehicles were sold all over Europe but not in the UK. Ford UK were building the Thames 400e, which was the best-selling van in the UK, while also exporting to parts of Europe and Canada, but not to Germany. Minibuses were very popular with buyers and Ford spent a large part of their advertising budget promoting them. Both vans were available to buy at the same time in showrooms all over Europe.

Both countries had their teams working on and testing the vans. Henry Ford Jr said he was amazed at the lack of co-operation between his Ford companies. Germany's prototype, shown left, confirms how old-fashioned ideas were at the time. The UK's prototype (the proposed Thames 800E) was not much better, but did have a slightly more modern look. Henry Ford Jr was shown both of these projects within a few days of each other and he put in place a program that would end the expense.

The first part of the program was to build two test bucks (test vehicles). The planning part of the program cost £10 million, a budget set by Henry Ford himself. The bucks were made up of a mismatch of parts from numerous vehicles, plus a wooden platform to get the seating position and general size of the van itself, making sure that an 8 x 4 in. sheet of plywood could lay flat between the wheel arches and that it would fit through the doors. Arthur Molyneaux oversaw the two bucks. Sadly the bucks themselves were lost, as were the German drawings and pictures from the same era. While Arthur was not happy with his vans, they served a purpose, and it was not until the full design team got together on 11 January 1960 that things started to change for the better. Within a very short time the project then started to come together.

Choosing Arthur Molyneaux, far right, project planner was an outstanding decision. With his attention to detail and meticulous nature, the planning project underwent inspection like no other vehicle before, and so the V-series program was born. Henry Ford returned to look at what the UK planning team had come up with and was amazed at what they had done. Luckily for the Transit, Arthur Molyneux had been due to start planning on the D-series truck, but was side-lined to the Redcap program on the insistence of Henry Ford himself.

I interviewed Arthur in 2014. He was so pleased to be with Transits once again and recalled his days with the project, while looking around the 1965 Transit that he himself had driven all those years before.

Testing Times 1960–1965

Testing was carried out in fifteen different countries, with cold weather testing in Norway and hot weather testing in Portugal. Track testing took place at Ford's famous Boreham Proving Grounds, where thousands of miles were accrued up and down the A roads as the M1 London end did not open until 1966. Speeding reports to the police resulted in the vans being stopped a number of times before an engineer visited the local police station to explain what the vans were doing. Ford was told in not so many words, 'It's not what are you doing,' but rather, 'We cannot catch you up, what's under the bonnet? A Spitfire engine?' After the visit the police left the drivers and engineers alone. Pictures show a hole in the sliding door rails and the wrong air filter – all from project Redcap trials.

Testing in Portugal was undertaken near a town called Estremoz. The engineers stayed on after the testing period to make sure the diesel-fronted grill worked properly, as this was a late addition. They also needed to make sure the Perkins engine was fit for the job and would not overheat.

Vigorous testing was done on the engine for hot weather testing but it was only when the team arrived back in the UK that it was discovered that the engine did not like damp weather. The pictures were taken by Graham Tofield, an engineer in late 1965, while carrying out tests on the front suspension and the new diesel grill in Estremoz. My thanks go out to his son, Paul, for his help.

After just eleven months the testing became more intense and more specialised every day as components were added and removed, such as seats, roof air vents, doors, locks, steering wheels and brakes. It was quickly realised it would never move forward unless components were redesigned and the vehicles were pushed harder than ever. All the old Thames and Zodiac parts were taken off of the test vehicles' list and completely new parts were made. However, at the same time, as the picture shows below, the D-series was underway and some new parts from this program were fitted as there were heavy-duty truck parts that were deemed suitable.

Doors needed to be bigger to incorporate the planner's load space design – it had to take a full sheet of 8 x 4 in. plywood lying flat. To get this idea to work, hinges needed to be stronger and the distance between the inside wheel arches had to be wider. Side loading doors were introduced for the first time and these could be on either side to give better access. Ridges were also put into the steel floor pan to make them stronger and to stop flexing and damage.

As the vehicle came together in 1963, simple things like bumpers were designed to wrap around the lower front wings and rear quarter panels to protect the vulnerability of this lower area. All the early prototypes had these chromed bumpers with longer end returns, but they were changed before June 1965. When being fitted on the test production line in May 1965, it was difficult to fit the bumpers without scratching the paintwork. The bumper design was altered with a shortened end return to make assembly easier. Due to the delay on agreeing this, no 1965 Transits had chrome bumpers or chrome wing mirrors. They were all 'Ermine white', with some bumpers being black depending on the van's body colour.

The hardest aspects for the engineering team to overcome were the one-piece up and over rear doors, and the front sliding doors and locks. The one-piece rear door needed to stay in place when open and needed to be light enough to be opened by one man. This was quite a problem, and all the engineers I spoke to admitted this was the biggest hurdle to overcome. The door was the largest ever fitted to a light commercial vehicle, so Ford decided to use two opening rear doors until the Transit was actually on sale, then looked into the problem again in more detail. Yet again, it was 1966 before this option was available. Back doors were tested by VG Print, a newspaper company.

As a result of the problems with the one-piece rear door, orders placed by the emergency services had to have two rear doors that would later be converted to one up and over door in late 1966. The team had to use car door locks from May 1965, when the first vans came off the line, until the newly designed locks were ready in the December 1965 Transits. Zodiac door locks were fitted, which had to be reversed so they would work when they were sticking out from the A-pillar and were not suitable for use. The police vans also changed sliding side doors for slam doors to overcome this problem. These locks were unsightly, much to the disgust of Vernon Preston's design team.

A problem the team had to overcome was flexing in the side panels. Before uncovering the problem, it was originally thought it was due to outside airflow. Roof vents were introduced but this only increased outside noise. Then, at a later stage, a small oblong hole was cut in both sides of the rear panels to let the airflow pass through the van. This worked and so two small grills were pressed into the sides of the van and inside covers were fitted. It was later discovered that one grill would have been sufficient, so this changed in 1969/70.

The team was aware of the need for a van with a nicer interior. Vernon wanted this, and was working on all these smaller projects as well as the main design.

As the team was busy working on safety aspects like seats and protecting the driver from sliding loads, the niceties would have to wait. The idea of a custom cab was talked about in May 1964 but never taken further due to cost restrictions and staying under the Redcap budget. Custom cabs came into play in February 1966 when the orders were pouring in, and it was obvious the Transit was going to be a success.

To keep costs down, optional extras like over riders were brought in after 1965. The camper van converters who were buying large amounts of Transit vans at the time wanted items factory fitted, but Ford resisted this due to large numbers of vans being sold and the plants having large expansion projects to increase productivity. As a result, a lot of campers left the plant in primer. To keep Ford's costs down even passenger seats were an optional extra on the first Transits, along with floor mats and headliners.

Early on, Henry Ford Jr had decided cost was an issue, so the team in the UK took a look at what Ford USA were doing with a view of maybe getting some ideas on design engineering. He was worried the new project might be too expensive per unit price. A prototype van was sent to the UK for the team to look at and drive, coming with instructions telling the team that the cost of selling the van in Europe must be the same per unit as the American Econoline.

The Redcap book (recapitalisation book) gave the project its name and it stuck right up until May 1965. Both the USA and the UK projects did have a similarity from 1965 until the 1980s, which is clear looking at the photos of the Mk 2 Transit (*above*) and Econoline (*below*). The team in the UK thought it was too heavy and outdated, but maybe Henry Ford Jr was right, as the Econoline was the best-selling van in America until the Transit took over in 2014. From the mid-1990s, Ford stopped investing in the Econoline and its fate was sealed. Brian Walker's classic Econoline (*below*) shows the similarities between the two vans. My thanks to my good friend Brian for all the Econoline pictures.

The first test vans off the line in late May 1965 were heavily used for press pictures before doing compatibility and engineering tests. Every opportunity was used to promote the name Transit and the brand Ford. The UK plants were being invested in, and to advertise these new buildings the Transit was photographed at these sites. The Transit was also featured alongside Ford's best-selling tractors at the Silsoe Research Institute (a tractor testing company in Bedford).

In April/May 1965 the first vans to be assembled were put together on a line set up at Ford's Langley plant near Heathrow Airport. These vehicles would be used for testing, primarily to check that all the parts would fit together in a production line environment, and that the line would work as far as assembly was concerned. As with all vehicles, some outside suppliers were used for items such as nuts and bolts, switches, locks, instrument panels and so on, as well as underbody and side panels. It was the first time all these items came together in one place and four to five vans were built; no minibuses or pick-ups, just short wheelbase (SWB) vans. These vans were all scrapped in August 1966.

On 9/10 July 1965, when the first production Transit came off the line, Ford concentrated on SWB vans only, with the other body styles waiting until October. No one-piece doors or chrome bumpers were available until 1966. The new Transits were lined up to make comparisons in quality. When testing these vans a major problem was found – the front beam axle had a hairline casting crack, making it necessary to make some design changes. About 2,000 of these beams were scrapped. The parts were improved and rigorously tested before fitting. Pictures show the first van and the first engine on the line at Langley.

Just before the release date, Brian Eckersley, a young member of the Transit team, got the job of doing a comparison test with one van produced in the UK and one from the Genk plant in Belgium. One had Bosch electrical parts while the other had Lucas. There were two different engines – the Cologne V4 and the Essex V4. One van used imperial measurements, the other metric. Brian spotted, in fact, that no name had been chosen for the Redcap project van. He reported back to Vernon Preston that the Genk van had 'Taunus Transit' on the back doors as a joke (it was a badge left over from the old van). Thus, 'Transit' was adopted. At a lunch in 2015 when Brian left the room, Vernon told me the Transit would never have had the name if young Brian had not spotted the badge, and he so should get the honour of having naming the Transit. I must say I agree.

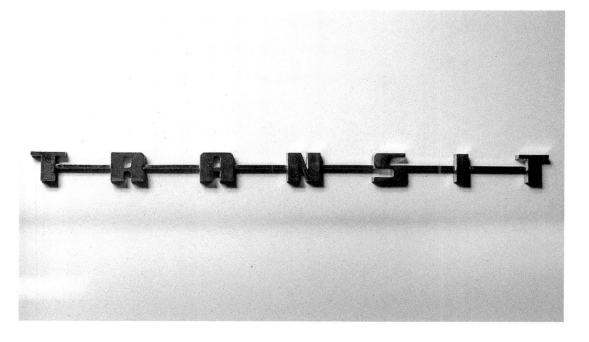

Production Time 1965–1978

The design of the Transit gave it the benefit of being very versatile, with orders from police to delivery vehicles for florist shops. No matter what type of body you wanted, the Transit could fit the bill. The speed at which the variations became available was amazing. Martin Walter campers had a delivery of thirty SWB panels in August 1965; Airborne Caravans had fifteen vans on 12 September. The parcel vans were on sale by January 1966. The SAS ordered ten vans delivered in March 1966, Lancashire Police had fifteen long wheelbase (LWB) vans in June, and fifty British Rail vans were delivered in December.

A big press release took place on 10 October 1965. After having talks across Europe with large fleet companies, Vernon Preston clinched two of the biggest orders for Transit within months – Teleboard in Norway and Seagas in the UK. These fleets of SVO vehicles were driving around showing Ford's new product. Not only did this kick-start sales, but it also boosted the name 'Transit'. In just months it took over from the outgoing Thames and became the best-selling van everywhere it was sold.

At this time, Transit's special vehicle options team were really busy. Based in a shed at the back of the Langley plant, the team had started working on variations of the van. New body styles were on the drawing boards before the Transit was even being sold. Along with chassis cab variations, the space-van (a parcel van coded the 10001) was under construction. The SVO shed was now home to some of the design team, who were thinking of even more ways to build the van and extend its popularity.

There was one part of the design that was missed until late in the process – diesel engines. The engine bay was designed for the V4 short block and there was no room for a bulky diesel engine. The diesel bumper needed to be redesigned. Ford tried bending the bumper as shown, but this was far too expensive, so they put it back on the drawing board and came up with an alternative, straighter bumper. This version was used to save costs as the diesel grill was not available until early 1966. The Perkins 4108 was fitted as well as small panels that fitted behind the bumper. As an added bonus for Ford, this grill and bonnet made it very easy to add the Essex V6 engine to the list of options available as an SVO option, making it very popular with the Emergency Services.

By 1966/67, different types of Transits were selling at an astonishing rate. Ford stated at the time, 'If there's a job, there's a Transit to do it.'

Ford supplied large fleets of ambulances and fire vans across Europe. It was the custom in northern Europe to have a small fire station or emergency building in towns and villages.

Campers, trucks and dustcarts were selling in every shape and size. Plants in the UK and Belgium started production of these SVO vehicles, with Turkey following in 1967.

Promoting the van was easy for Ford with the dealer set-up and contacts in the industry. They set up a 'Press and Dealer Week' in the press garage at head office and invited everyone. It was the biggest event Ford had ever put on to promote a vehicle in Europe. Company directors and the European press attended, along with car salesmen to show off the product and its attributes. The event was a great success.

Heavy loads were no problem for the Transit, and in a lot of cases made use of trailers. But also vans were starting to carry things you would never believe, as companies like Chassis Developments in Luton started to build ever more impressive bodies on the Transit. Companies would spend four times more on the body than the van itself. Transits even ran on railway tracks in some countries.

The campervan companies were very fast to take up the option of ordering Transits in large numbers, ordering up to 9 per cent of vans built in 1968. This included the single- and twin-wheeled Transit chassis cab. The Sprite, Autosleeper and Jennings conversions led the way, using twin- and single-wheelers. Martin Walter were the main dealers for single-wheeled camper vans. Ford at the time did look into building these for themselves, but decided to leave it to outside coachbuilders to undertake this work. However, some campers built by outside companies were on sale in Ford dealerships and carried a Ford warranty.

Large and small Transit-based campers were soon available but these were not cheap, and self-build versions soon took off with kits being made available. It opened up European countries as affordable destinations for families. In fact at the dealer launch in late 1965 a camper was on show, built by Airborne Caravans (based in Southend-on-Sea). As Ford got the plants sorted out they started producing custom cab Transits like the high spec Freedom. At the same time Ford had introduced new paint colours, like Ambassador Blue. This 1966 camper (*above*) is owned by Stewart Waldron. It is one of the very rare vans, the high quality build has helped the vehicle survive to the present day. Built in April 1966, it was one of the first Freedom vans produced at Langley.

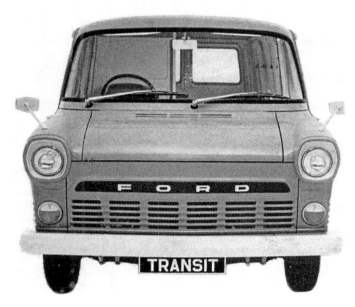

While some changes had been made in 1969, in 1971 Ford changed the look of the Transit, giving it a more car-like oval grill (*below*). Among the updates were seats, switches, and servo-assisted direct action breaks with better foot pedals and bigger wing mirrors. Together with the crash pad on the dashboard, new back light assembly, push button radio, and a new 2.4 litre diesel engine, the badges on the back doors also changed so you could identify the models easier. The suspension was also changed to minimal leaf type. However, behind the driver zone the load space doors and basic shape of the van stayed the same.

Designers were looking at every option to increase sales, including the very rare bathtub pickup. This van (*above*) was tested but after some work it was dropped although a few were sold in Europe and South Africa. The minibus side of things resulted in a great deal of money being spent on market research that paid off as sales rose 10 per cent over the next three years. Aircraft travel was becoming popular and getting to and from airports gave the Transit another job.

Minibuses had become quite big in Europe with the twenty-two-window panorama built at Genk as well as in the UK, as schools and mini-cab firms started to purchase them. Soon people wanted to travel in style and Ford took advantage of this. In 1976, the Transit minibus accounted for 7 per cent of the vehicles being made. Today these early minibuses are the rarest vans to find as they did not last due to the high mileage they did and working in all weathers. Thank you to my friend Peter Brown for the use of his picture.

Time for a Change 1978–1986

Vast amounts of money was spent promoting the Mk 2 Transit in the first week of production. Newspaper coverage featured in even the smallest local papers. At the same time, huge press events were held all around Europe in late 1977. The first press drive day was 6 February 1978 at Castle Combe, and the first van was off the line on 21 February.

The Mk 1 steering wheel was prone to deterioration due to the heat that was projected through the windscreen in the summer. It got extremely hot and would crack. The old dash mat was removed as this was made of leatherette material and would also suffer. In an effort to overcome this problem, extensive research was done on the steering wheel and dash over a three-year period and a completely new steering wheel and dash were fitted to the van in 1978.

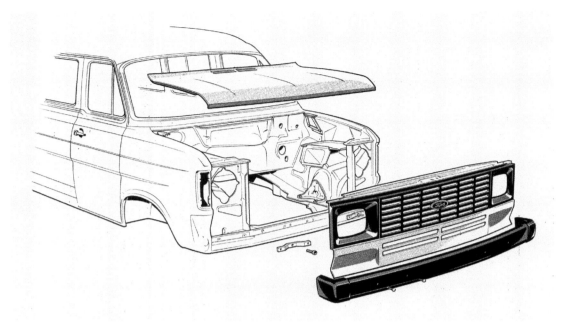

Ford had been testing a new type of Transit for four years, and it was released in July 1977. Known as the 77 Half Transit, it had a front grill facelift, so didn't qualify as having a completely new front end but it did have some other changes to other panels. It was sent for testing at Lommel Proving Ground and by this time Ford's tried and tested combination of hard driving in both cold and hot countries was working well.

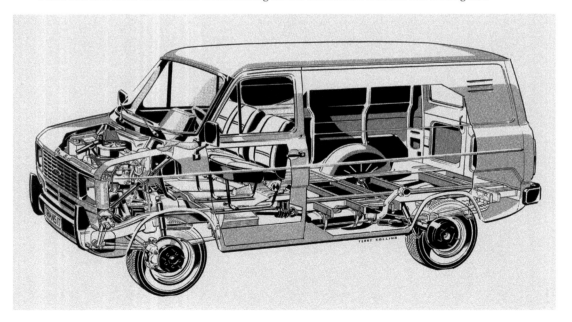

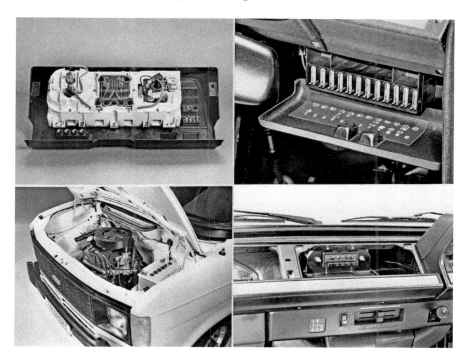

Now with a completely new cab, numerous changes in safety and comfort were also made. Included in the alterations were a more refined front end, a plastic dash, new 1.6 and 2 litre petrol and 2.4 diesel engines plus the new C3 auto box. The floor had been changed, and there was now a two-speed heater and better cab insulation. More upgrades included the bigger, self-adjusting brakes with anti-corrosion warranty, as well as to the instrument cluster, fuse box and gearbox, improved access to the fuse panel, longer service times, better MPG, new rear lights and new front headlights. Finally, for the first time the most popular colour choice for the Transit was white.

The load space for the Mk 2 was the same as the 1965 Mk 1 model, but changes had been made to the door handles and locks, along with a new wiring loom and front and rear lights. More countries around the world were now selling the Transit, including Russia, Australia, Portugal, Turkey and Belgium, just to name a few. By this stage Transit had become a name people knew. Celebrities were happy to put their name to the brand, including Roy Castle (*below*). By July 1980, the LWB had become the best seller instead of the SWB.

Meanwhile in the USA (where testing was carried out in the Arizona desert from 1977 to 1979), an interesting change happened in the way information was gathered. The National Street Van Association in the USA carried out a public opinion poll to see if the Transit would interest American van drivers. Two vans were at a 'Truckin' event in Farmington, Missouri, in July 1977, where Fred Blumenthal organised a van driver's poll on behalf of Ford Motor Company to see if the van owners liked the new van. These polls were also carried out in Europe to see what the public thought of the new van and it was a resounding success. My thanks to my good friend Fred for the pictures.

At this time groups of teenage van drivers started to form clubs. These clubs were not only made up of Ford vans, but due to the availability of Ford models they were quite prominent within these groups around the world. Ford were very quick to take up this challenge and made a number of specialist vehicles around the world to show they were up to date with the latest trends. One person who was building vans at this time was Steve Stringer, and he became the top name in custom van projects in the UK. Steve worked on both the Mk 1 and Mk 2 Transit vans to produce his works of art and made appearances at all the big shows of the day in the UK and Europe.

Ford produced custom vans in the USA, Germany, and Australia.

As Ford took the Transit into the 1980s, promotion was the name of the game and Ford's marketing department went into overdrive. The Transit was advertised in every way possible, from television adverts to magazines, newspapers, and full-sized van-shaped printed displays. The successful project Supervan 1 had passed into history, making way for Supervan 2. With its F1 engine and sleek lines, it was to be a real head-turner. This replica Transit van was made on a 1/7th scale out of fiberglass. It turned heads wherever it appeared and was built by an outside contractor. When it was known that Supervan 2 was going to make an appearance at any race circuit or show, the gate attendance would go up by 25 per cent. The 178-mph van was a real success for Ford.

Variations of Transits on the road had expanded a lot by 1980; if something could be fitted on the back of a van, it was. Companies converting Transits grew tenfold between 1978 and 1986. The cost of a standard SWB panel Transit van was £2,768 but this price could triple with the added conversion costs. The tow truck (*above*) was a very popular design and one-off conversions were also popular, like the police camera van (*left*). Over 200 extras could be added to your SVO van at the plant when ordering, from springs to a double passenger seat. Bright colours were also the order of the day. For the first time, bright red and bright yellow, along with white, were the top colours ordered.

In 1983 Ford gave the Transit another facelift. The obvious difference was the plastic grill, as opposed to the steel grill. The new plastic grill gave less drag and wind noise and was easier to remove to work within the engine bay. Ford always looked at these facelifts long and hard before undertaking expensive tests, so artists and clay modellers were used at the start of the process.

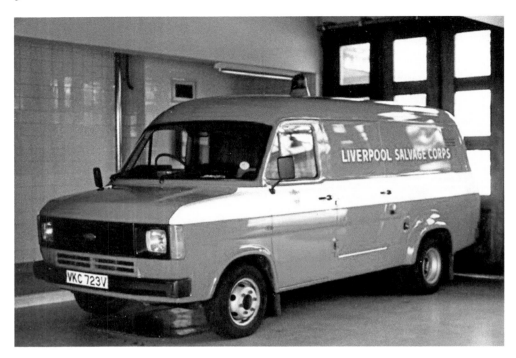

These new grilled vans (*below*) had the award-winning 2.5 litre Di diesel engine fitted, which gave it greatly improved performance. It had been in Europe for nearly a year by the time it was added to the UK line-up and fitted with the new grill. This change to the model was well-received by the press and was reported as changes to the already perfect van. A twelve-month parts and labour warranty was introduced, a first in the marketplace, and the overdrive gearbox was now an option. Other changes include two-speed washer wipers, a three-speed heater and the dash was now a light grey. The brakes were also upgraded with microwave-timed brakeless ignition. Seat options were also different, with vinyl seats in the standard van and fabric seats in the custom.

The plastic-grilled Mk 2 Transit was only on sale for around three years before a completely new model was released. Although sales of this facelift sold well, the grill proved to be a bit fragile and harder to remove than the previous steel grill. However, the other updates had more than made up for this one problem. The overdrive gearbox was a great success, as were the new bumpers and front spoiler (still highly sought-after items today). Ford also introduced the factory-built pickup truck, which was very popular. Thanks to my friend Mark for the picture of his rare LWB van.

A Change of Direction
1986–1995

For the first time since 1965, twenty-one years before, a new Transit was on the road. No punches were pulled as a full campaign got underway. Ford publicised the new Mk 3 on 2 December 1985 with a week-long campaign for the first time. It was TV- and radio-based, while the newspapers and magazine coverage took a back seat. Also, as a bit of a twist, you could walk into your dealership and get a free model of the new van in a nice Ford box.

In 1985 the prototype Mk 3 had finished being tested and was ready to launch. For the first time computers were taking part in Ford's tests in an effort to find new ways of designing the perfect vehicle. The engineering team leader, Peter Nevetts, was very advanced in his way of looking at design. Peter was the first Ford designer to look at the advancement of computer technology as a way of development and designing. The new prototype van underwent testing in Portugal for van loading and heat tests. Peter introduced the old Portuguese load testing idea back into the program but this time with changes. Water bottles were filled with liquid until they reached the specified weight, tested for 100 miles, and then emptied to test the unloaded weight on the return journey. Long-distance 24-hour tests were once again carried out at Ford's Lommel Proving Grounds, and the hot and cold weather testing happened in Norway and the USA.

An outside French company came up with a design for the Mk 3 Transit, although this work only incorporated design, with no engineering plans. Their design was refused, as Ford viewed it as old fashioned and not the way Ford wanted to carry the Transit forward. Ford's own design team took charge of the project at Dunton. Peter Nevett's team (*below*) went on to design the Mk 3 and for the first time asked fleet buyers to road test the prototypes. They used them for every-day deliveries in the normal working environment. A total of 450 changes were implemented due to this program being put in place. When the van was first put on sale it was apparent that Ford had taken the Transit to new levels as sales of the new van broke all expectations.

With the new, heavier platform, it was possible to focus on the load and carrying capacity. Ford made the Transit bigger to carry all sorts of materials and the Transit High Cube was born. These vans could only be built by aftermarket companies or at Genk due to the low roof height at the plant in Southampton. At the same time (which became a plus for Ford) these vans had a really high re-sale price and Ford, being unable to meet supply at one stage, had a one year purchase waiting list.

Between models, Ford's designers and engineers were also looking at other ways to build innovations on the Transit body. This was accomplished by involving apprentices to come up with ideas. One such design they were working on was a project that really did look like something from the future. The use of the RS logo on the Escort race car worked extremely well. The project never did get to the roadworthy stage, but became very popular with the press and Transit van fans, who still have a fondness for this project thirty years later. It was transported to Lommel for the photo shoot (*below*) after being moved from Ford's design centre at Dunton.

In 1991/2 it was time again for another facelift, with the introduction of the Mk 4. This model had been worked on as early as 1987 but for the first time European laws affected changes, two of which were chassis strength and lighting. Ford did an enormous amount of work to get the van just right by involving outside companies and making technical and engineering changes to stay up to date with what drivers wanted and EU laws required.

The big change was power assisted steering. The front grill was changed slightly and both driver's and passenger seats were updated with lumber support. It had a Lucas Epic engine management system (thanks to Peter Nevetts), anti-lock brakes were fitted as standard – an industry first – and the Euro gas emissions system fitted in line with European regulations. Yet again the press and public loved the new additions to the Transit and the improved drive that the power assisted steering gave them. Transit was in its twenty-seventh year as the top-selling van and was smashing all records for sales.

Running costs were becoming a focus for van drivers and advertising made sure people were aware of the new engines. Ford offered four engines in 1993: the 1.6 OHC; the 2.0 OHC; the diesel 2.5 Di; and an SVO engine, the 100PS 3Ltr V6. All four were tried and tested. The V6 was also offered in the chassis cab and used in vehicles like transporters, police vans, ambulances, and vans for the AA and RAC. In some cases vibration was a problem with the Di engine, so the MacPherson strut suspension was fitted at planning stages to all Mk 4 vans. This acted as a dampener effect and reduced both noise and vibration.

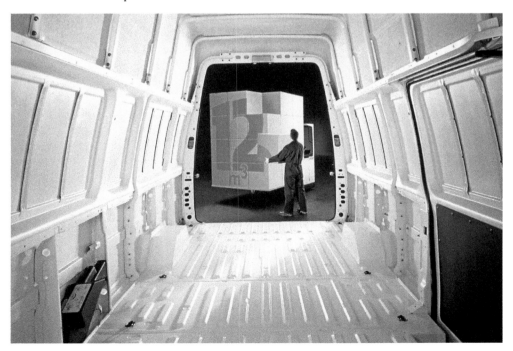

Peter Nevetts' Mk 3 and Mk 4 Transit were game changers for Ford. Innovation linked with engineering and design excellence made these the vans that took Transit into the future. It made a Transit van that could go anywhere and put Ford in a position that other manufacturers only dreamed of. To get out of a Mk 2 and into a Mk 3 or Mk 4 was like moving from a wheelbarrow into a spaceship. The ideas that came from these two Transit models, once again, changed the industry. Ford's very close contacts with outside contractors, engineering programs and innovation seemed to be endless.

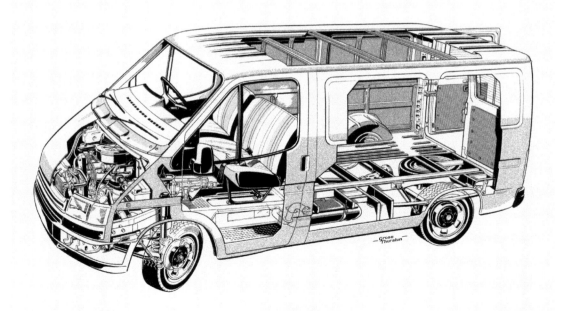

The Smiley-Faced Transit
1995–2000

The Mk 5 was yet another facelift. It achieved a large following mainly because it changed things so much and became recognised in its own way as a new van. Loved by the public, it was immediately known as the 'smiley-faced Transit'. It came with six new engines – four diesel and two petrol – as well as a new dash, new minibus seating with advanced seating positions (an industry first), and all-round lap belts to all seats in minibuses. Also introduced was a better dealer network. The larger High Cube vans could hold 12 square metres of goods in the back.

The Tourneo minibus was a great addition to the Transit line-up. This range is still running today; with its high standard of finish to the interior, twelve- and fifteen-seat options and car-like feel, it has added to the trust people have in the brand. It had a new climate control system along with lower Euro emissions, and air vents were brought back from the 1965 Transit to help rear ventilation in the load space.

To commemorate 30 years of their success, Ford made a limited edition panel van called the Hallmark. It had all available options and was exclusively built at Southampton; 600 in total, in three colours. Today these vans have become a collector's item. The model was instantly added to Ford's heritage fleet – a position it still holds today.

As part of the 1995 '30 years' celebration', Ford did a very large advertising campaign with lots of photo shoots. This included Supervan 2, which had some changes along with a new smiley-faced grill fitted onto the earlier vehicle. Gone was the square front end and the new aerodynamic front end was fitted. It was painted in new Ford colours and the transformation was quite dramatic. Ford also brought out their heritage fleet to promote the anniversary, together with a host of memorabilia for collectors and Transit fans. A photoshoot was held at Abbey Road outside the studios at 5 a.m. to make a brochure and poster to promote thirty years of Transit being number one.

The Mk 5 advertising went on all year and was by far the largest campaign Ford had ever undertaken to promote the Transit. The hard work of the design team was apparent with lots of extras, including a new dash, designed to be driver friendly, and seating comfort; one aspect that Ford promoted in particular this time around. Metallic paint was offered as well and also, for the first time in vehicle history, 87 per cent of this new van was recyclable.

The new smiley-faced Transit brought forward all the great things from the updated Mk 4 that had been released just a few years before. At the time Ford used a slogan that stated 'The delivery system of the 90s', and that was the case as sales increased with the introduction of the MT75 gearbox across the whole line. It had self-adjusting ABS brakes, Ford's award-winning Di engine and the new 2 litre 115PS petrol engine (that even met car emission standards). Also included was 10-inch brake booster for better braking, optional air-con, central locking, new high back seats, larger door pockets and a heater that had doubled its capacity since the Mk 4 Transit. It also had a larger rear door and a two-stage alarm so you could lock all the doors or just some of them.

A Van for the New Century
2000–2005

The engineering team in the Arizona desert, hot weather testing the prototype 2000 Transit in 1998.

The Mk 6 Transit was launched in 2000, primarily designed in the USA, with the design team from Dunton in Essex being flown out to Ford's head office in Dearborn and living in and around the facility. Clay model work had been underway for a few years prior to the move and this also involved the outside company Hawtal Whitings, in California. For the first time the Transit was going to be truly international and not just from a testing point of view. Testing was carried out in Belgium, Arizona and the Arctic Circle.

It was Ford's policy to test with outside companies like UPS, who were using the vans on loan and reporting back to Ford on their performance. That proved very successful and paved the way for the Transit being built and sold in the USA over ten years later. The launch of the Mk 6 was an enormous event with 26,000 dealers, press and Ford employees being taken to Seville in Spain in late 1999 to drive the new van. The design team were very proud of the changes. The new Transit had three Duratorq engines, keyless van entry, lockable bonnet, self-adjusting clutch, larger front discs for better stopping distance, drive by wire, ABS, driver airbags, in-cab battery for longer life, front- and rear-wheel drive and two load space heights for easier loading.

Front- and rear-wheel drive options were added and this led to a boom in Transit conversions, with available models doubling in just eighteen months. Be it twin cabs, dustcarts, box vans or jumbos, the options were endless. A point that is still true today: any owner/driver could get the Transit that fitted his needs perfectly. Minibuses were an important factor of this growth. Along with a five-speed box, the new Transit was cleaner; it had a water-cooled exhaust gas recirculation (EGR) system, servicing intervals were now 18,000 miles and the van was lighter than the previous models, giving better MPG.

Ford put together a drivers' day to celebrate forty years of Transit in 2005. Owner/drivers and fleet customers took part, with 275 vans in convoy from Dunton to Southampton, and then a big birthday party to celebrate.

The Transit Van Club helped to arrange a number of birthday parties, attended by drivers around the country from Southampton to Liverpool. With the Transit selling in larger numbers than ever before, it made the perfect platform for Ford celebrating their flagship van. These parties were put on all over Europe by owners, drivers, companies and Ford garages. Transit had, by this stage, become more than a van, but the byword for a product that fits the needs of the person driving it. The word 'icon' was used for the first time by the press declaring, 'You can't design an icon, it had to earn that badge'.

 THE VERSATILE FORD TRANSIT RANGE

New changes were updated ABS brakes, all-round driver and passenger airbags (as well as side airbags), Isofix child seat fixings and increased and improved crash test results. It was also possible to lock all, or just some, doors. High-level alarm and trailer monitoring and the heavy-duty front axle 150AH was introduced for ambulances as an SVO option. Ford also introduced two extra levels of interior fittings – the LX and the GLX – giving drivers the chance to choose their perfect environment. Under the SVO banner there were 130 options, excluding special colours. This new van was as technically advanced as it possibly could be at the time, with the lighting and emissions meeting European laws.

Ford designers and artists have been hard at work since 1995, looking at the best way to take the Transit forward from an exterior point of view. Showing the best of what Ford designers had in their minds at the time is very interesting, and from the pictures you can extract small design aspects and details of what they were thinking. Some of the details do turn up a few years later in the real Transit vans on our roads.

In 2007 Ford released the Transit Sports Van in Performance Blue, with only 1,000 of these first Sports vans advertised. It soon caught on, helped by celebrities like Sabine Schmitz of *Top Gear* fame. Leather interiors and a 140 psi engine made this van a great success and led to a number of the vans being produced in new colours over the next few years. However, the specifications changed to cloth interiors and 130 psi engines. While all the Sports vans were made in Southampton, some prototype interiors were built in left-hand drive German vans. Both the Transit Connect and Fiesta Sports Van were also on sale at this time. The introduction of these models changed the way Ford looked at the van and these vans were the first in a long run of custom-type vans that are still on sale today in the Transit family line-up.

The Jumbo was selling extremely well with the introduction of the 3.5-ton Transit. Fleet orders made up a big percentage of sales and emergency services were taking up the Transit as their vehicle of choice. Ford's long-lasting company policy of paying particular attention to special vehicle options (SVO) was paying dividends. Things like the 'All-wheel drive option' and the 'Van of the Year' trophy all added to the name of Transit. Introduction of parking aids, rain sensing windscreen wipers and automatic headlights (the industry's first) added to the long list of options available. Fire, police and ambulance Transits require a high level of SVO additional fittings before being shipped to outside conversion companies. Some of these items can only be fitted in the Ford plants.

In 2010, for the forty-fifth birthday of the Transit, Ford got long-time Ford fans to attend the event. Henry Cooper was first pictured with his Mk 1 Transit in 1965, standing proudly with a bunch of bananas to promote his greengrocer's shop in Wembley. At the time he was driving a Transit in and around the area to get the shop off the ground; since that date that picture has been used for over fifty-two years by newspapers and magazines. Ford had the idea of getting Henry to re-enact this photo, not only with a Mk 1 Transit (owned by Phil Gassor at the time) but also with a new Sports van. This picture made an instant success of the press day with the newspapers and TV. Henry's first picture is the most used picture the press office ever took of the Transit, closely followed by elephants in a van.

The Transit Family
2005–2014

The new Ford Family line-up. Four vans under one name – Transit.

The Transit world was turned upside down in 2012 when Ford announced the introduction of the Transit family four. The idea was that every van driver should have a van that fitted his or her requirements, be it large or small; a van for every customer from large to small and all built with the environment in mind. Drivers would no longer be driving around in a large Transit with a few boxes in the back or driving around in a small overloaded van. The first of these to arrive was the Transit Custom. There was now a Transit for every business.

The design and testing of the Transit Custom, a completely new vehicle, was extreme even by Ford's standards. Testing took every aspect of the van to new heights of excellence. While a lot of this work was carried out under computer-controlled environments around the world, it was also tested to destruction on roads and at Lommel, where it had six months of 24/7 driving with drivers changing over every two hours, driving the vans 5 million kilometres non-stop. At Dunton lots of tests took place, including the slamming of doors a quarter of a million times. In all this new Transit was tested in Dubai, South Africa, Italy (for hot weather testing) performance testing in Austria and South Africa and Norway at -40 °C (for cold weather testing) by the time it reached the public.

The new Transit Custom drive was a whole new experience for van drivers, giving them a real car-like drive, even when fully loaded, while at the same time giving a feel of luxury only normally found in high-end vehicles. It won 'International Van of the Year' in 2013 and had phone connectability with Ford's new SYNC program. For the first time in forty-seven years, other companies stopped their design projects due to the new Custom and had to re-think what they were doing. A total of 10,000 orders were placed in the UK before a single van had even been built, and that was only panel vans. There were also orders for the double cab, Kombi, Tourneo and ECOnetic vans as well. Over the next few years the Custom would be given more than ten industry awards, including a maximum five-star NCAP safety award.

The second member of the Transit family, the Mk 3 Transit Connect (as the early design picture shows), was always going to be a winner. It hit the streets in 2013, winning the accolade of 'Van of the Year' in 2014. With the Transit Custom taking the market by storm, the new Connect's first showing was at the Paris Motor Show in September 2012. People were ready to order the new Transit as soon as it went on sale. The replacement for the old 2002 Connect (that was updated in 2007) was a completely new vehicle in every way. Deemed the perfect small van, it had eye-catching styling and design, while also being very easy to drive. Being the perfect environment for any person to carry out their daily drive, but also having the technology to turn the van into a workplace when parking by the roadside, it soon got the nickname 'Office on Wheels'.

Mk 8 Lifting the Bar 2014

The new full-sized Transit van came out in 2014 and, like all new Transits, had all the gadgets that people expected it to have, while at the same time maintaining the name for design and practicality. Long-distance testing was carried out in Belgium. It was sold in the USA for the first time (as the old Ford Econoline van was being phased out). It was now built in Kansas City at Ford's established van plant. Designed in Essex at the Dunton studios, it was the first time 3D printing had been used in earnest to cut down the design process and costs.

2015 was '50 Years of Transit' and Ford held major events to commemorate the birthday, as did the press with over fifteen national newspapers, eight major TV programmes and numerous magazines. By this time the Transit Courier had been released, completing the Transit family of vans. Transit had been the number one selling van in the UK, and now holds that honour in the USA and other parts of Europe as well. Eight million vans have already been sold and this number is rising every week by large numbers.

If you wanted to buy a Transit you had over 450 types of Transit to choose from. The list was endless, from a panel van to a truck with all the options: cruise control, lane keeping alert, rear view camera, all-wheel drive, static cornering lights, tyre pressure monitoring, ESC (so if you took a corner too fast it would help correct the driver). The new 2-ton Transit had a two year warranty or 30,000 miles. There were changes from the UK to the USA, with the van's auto box and low roofline being the two that stand out. The auto box was offered in the UK in 2017 after nearly three years of testing in America. The low top Transit (*below*) was only available in the USA with the medium and high top being available worldwide.

The Mk 8 Transit was now a real world-beater and was selling in larger numbers than ever. You had the choice of FWD, RWD or all-wheel drive. It could tow 3.5 tons and had a load space of over 15 cubic metres, and introduced a car-like steering wheel, great seating, and all the added extras like sat nav, air-conditioning and reversing cameras. This time Ford released the DViC chassis cab in October 2014. Sales figures showed they sold nearly 66,000 full-sized 2-ton Transits in 2013 and sold nearly 16,000 vans in October 2016 alone. Design model and prototype work was carried out in the UK.

The Transit Courier was the last of the family to be announced by Ford. This does not resemble a car in any way from an engineering point of view, but drive it and it's just like a car. Loaded or unloaded the Courier was a tough little machine, just waiting to do any job just like the full-sized Transit and, yet again, safety, design and practicality were the order of the day.

In April 2017, the new automatic six-speed Transaxle gearbox was introduced to the full-sized Transit as well as the Custom, along with the new air suspension on the passenger-carrying Custom. In January, Ford announced the first fleets participating in a trial with the Met Police, TfL, British Gas, Addison Lee, and Clancy Plant. All will be using a plug-in Hybrid Transit. It is a twenty-vehicle trial lasting twelve months, supported by Transport for London. The consumer vehicles are planned for mass production in 2019. The London trial is to work directly with consumers to see if it works for them, and then the production vehicle based on the findings in 2019. My thanks to Ford director Mark Harvey, who is the face of Ford for the electrified van program based at Dunton.

Ford are working all the time on new Transits (always five years ahead), be it with technical or design advancement, or a new facelift grill. Ford are still using clay models and incorporating new advances into the Transit. The process never seems to stop, and as things move forward, computers give designers more power to project their images onto a screen straight from their minds. The sky's the limit.

Now the Transit has become a world-beater in every sense of the word; Ford are selling more vans than any other company in the world. The low roof Transit that is sold in the USA, could that turn up in Europe? The Transit Custom seen in the rest of the world could go to the USA, or may we see a Supervan 4 perhaps? Driverless vans in Dearborn are already being tested and hydrogen vans are testing at Lommel. After working and playing with Transits for over forty-eight years, I know better than to guess.

Into the Future

Here are some of the designs Ford are working on at the moment. In a few years' time, when the new Transit family is on the road, take the time to look and see just how near to the real thing these become. Only time will tell how far Ford will take the best-selling van in the world.

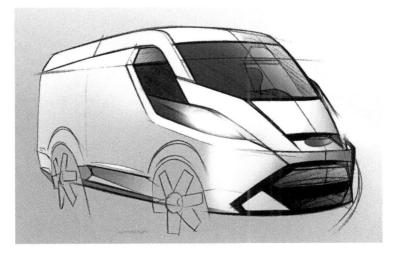

There will be a new face-lift Transit at the end of 2017 with full-sized clay models sitting in Dunton's design studio, waiting for the decision as to whether to go ahead or re-design new ideas again. But you can bet it will not be just a new grill. Face-lifts are never just a new grill – they always come with a long list of updates and new engineering wonders to keep the Transit up to date. If the latest artwork is anything to go by, it could be a very special.

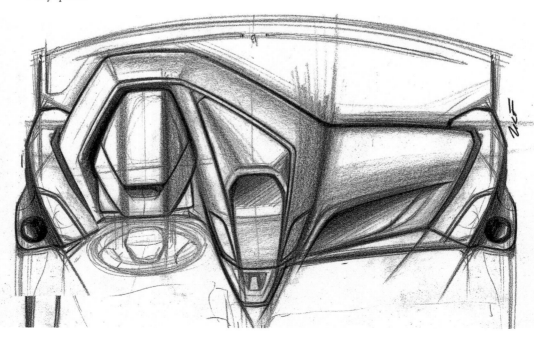

Colin Gray (left) and Ivan at the Ford heritage centre with the 1965 GEC Transit. Colin's knowledge and love of the Ford Oval and in particular the Transit was amazing, and he always had a smile and a kind word. RIP Colin, you will be missed by so many people.

Acknowledgements

I would like to thank my friends for the use of their pictures. Without their help in putting this book together it would not have been possible. Their enthusiasm is infectious and keeps me going. Thank you Colin Gray, Fred Blumenthal, Brian Walker, Peter Brown, Barry Gale, Brian Eckersley, Ivan Bartholomeusz and Paul Tofield for the great pictures his father, Graham, took in 1965. Thanks also to my family, for putting up with my Transit obsession for the last forty-five years, and also my grandchildren, George, Charlotte, William, and the new addition to the family, Luna. My thanks to Natasha, for doing the editing, Ford Motor Company, for all their support over the years, Mark Oakley and Stuart Waldron, for being my support team / technical advisors and for keeping my fleet on the road, and last but not least my wife Debi, who has lived with me and my 22,000 Transit items without one complaint for over twenty years.